SCIENCE CORNER

Water

Alice Harman

WAYLAND

Explore the world with **Popcorn -** your complete first non-fiction library.

Look out for more titles in the Popcorn range. All books have the same format of simple text and striking images. Text is carefully matched to the pictures to help readers to identify and understand key vocabulary.
www.waylandbooks.co.uk/popcorn

First published in 2013 by Wayland
Copyright © Wayland 2013

Wayland
Hachette Children's Books
338 Euston Road
London NW1 3BH

Wayland Australia
Level 17/207 Kent Street
Sydney NSW 2000

 Produced for Wayland by
White-Thomson Publishing Ltd
www.wtpub.co.uk
+44 (0)843 208 7460

Editor: Alice Harman
Designer: Clare Nicholas
Picture researcher: Alice Harman
Series consultant: Kate Ruttle
Design concept: Paul Cherrill

British Library Cataloguing in Publication Data
Harman, Alice.
   Water. -- (Science corner)(Popcorn)
   1. Water--Juvenile literature.
   I. Title II. Series
   546.2'2-dc23

ISBN: 978 0 7502 7761 7

Wayland is a division of Hachette Children's Books,
an Hachette UK company.
www.hachette.co.uk

Printed and bound in China

Picture/illustration credits:
Peter Bull 23; Stefan Chabluk 8–9; Dreamstime:
Feng yu 14tl; Getty: Justin Sullivan 21; Shutterstock:
Ronald Summers cover, holbox 4, anyaberkut 5, Wild
Arctic Pictures 6, Andrew Astbury 7, Balint Sebestyen
10, Dr. Morley Read 11, rm 12, Mikhail Markovskiy
13, rm 14tr, Achimdiver 14b, Maxim Tupikov 15t,
SJ Watt 15b, Jamie Duplass 16, 3445128471 18,
corepics 19, Stephane Bidouze 20; WaterAid: Rindra
Ramasomanana.

Every effort has been made to clear copyright.
Should there be any inadvertent omission,
please apply to the publisher for rectification.

Contents

Water on Earth   4

Ice   6

The water cycle   8

Rivers   10

Waterfalls and lakes   12

Animals   14

Drinking water   16

How we use water   18

Water pollution   20

True or false?   22

Make a rain gauge   23

Glossary   24

Index   24

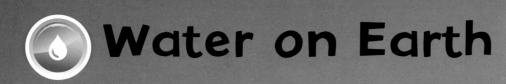

Water on Earth

Most of planet Earth is covered with water.
The oceans hold almost all of this water.
They are very wide and deep.

Boats can sail across the ocean to countries that are very far away.

Plants and animals need water to live. People drink water, and plants take water from the soil.

If there is not a lot of rain, we have to water plants.

Ice

At the north and south of the
Earth, there are huge areas of ice.
This frozen water partly melts in
the summer.

Arctic foxes change colour.
They match the white ice
in winter, and the brown
ground in summer.

A glacier is a huge area of ice and snow. It moves slowly over the land.

Glaciers contain one third of the world's fresh water.

Franz Josef Glacier in New Zealand starts high up in the mountains.

The water cycle

Water from the land and ocean
rises up through the air as vapour.
This water vapour makes clouds.

The water falls from the clouds as rain and snow. It flows into the land and ocean, and the water cycle starts again.

rain

river

lake

Rivers

The start of the river is called its source. Most rivers start high in the mountains or hills.

Tiny streams of water join together to form a river.

Rivers get bigger as more streams flow into them. Mud, stones and soil are carried along by the river. This makes the water look less clear.

The Amazon River can be so muddy that people cannot see anything in it.

The Amazon River in South America runs through seven countries.

11

Waterfalls and lakes

As rivers flow downhill, they sometimes pass over steep rocks. The water falls through the air until it hits the ground again. This falling river is called a waterfall.

The highest waterfall in the world is Angel Falls in Venezuela.

Some rivers run into lakes. Lakes are large areas of water that have land around them. Water often flows out of lakes and continues on to the sea.

Lake Baikal in Russia is the deepest lake in the world.

● Animals

Almost half of all types of animal on Earth live in the oceans. The water in the oceans is salty.

Watch out! Some jellyfish have long tentacles that can sting you.

The blue whale is the biggest animal on Earth.

Sea turtles can live for over 200 years.

Many animals live in and around freshwater rivers and lakes. Fresh water is not salty like the ocean.

Piranhas live in rivers in South America. They have very sharp teeth.

Hippos can run faster than any human in the world!

Drinking water

In most towns and cities, running water comes from lakes and rivers. The water is cleaned before we use it.

You should try to drink 1 litre (four glasses) of water a day.

Drinking fountains give us fresh, clean water.

There is clean water deep underground. People dig holes called wells, and bring up this water to drink.

Water pumps make it easier to take water out of wells.

How we use water

We use water at home to wash ourselves, cook food, clean clothes, flush the toilet and for many other things.

You can save water by turning off the tap while you brush your teeth!

Leaving the tap on while brushing your teeth wastes 12 litres of water every day.

Many factories use lots of water to make things such as computers, paper, food and cars. Cold water cools machines, which can get very hot.

Factories can recycle water so that they don't use too much of it.

Water pollution

Water pollution happens when people throw rubbish into rivers, lakes and seas. This rubbish can poison the water so it is not safe to drink.

Plastic bottles are the most common cause of water pollution.

Always recycle your bottles! Only 1 in 10 plastic bottles are recycled.

Oil is transported on huge ships.
Sometimes these ships are damaged,
and oil flows into the ocean.
Animals and plants are hurt.

This person is helping to clean oil off a bird.

True or false?

The right answer to all of the true or false questions below can be found in this book. Try to remember what the answers are, and look in the book if you really don't know.

1. Fresh water is salty.
True or **false**?

2. Angel Falls is the highest waterfall in the world.
True or **false**?

3. Clouds are made of water vapour.
True or **false**?

4. The source is the beginning of a river.
True or **false**?

5. Glaciers move very quickly.
True or **false**?

6. Humans and animals can stay alive without water.
True or **false**?

Answers: 1 = false, 2 = true, 3 = true, 4 = true, 5 = false, 6 = false.

Make a rain gauge

You will need:
a clean, empty large plastic bottle · scissors · sticky tape · water · waterproof pen · ruler

A rain gauge can show how much rain has fallen in a day, a week or a month.

1. Ask an adult to cut the top off the plastic bottle where the slope begins. Turn the top upside down inside the bottle, and stick it in place.

2. Fill the bottom of the bottle with a little bit of water. Mark the point that the water reaches as 0 cm.

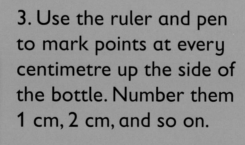

3. Use the ruler and pen to mark points at every centimetre up the side of the bottle. Number them 1 cm, 2 cm, and so on.

20
19
18
17
16
15
14
13
12
11
10
9
8
7
6
5
4
3
2
1
0

4. Leave your rain gauge outside where it can catch the raindrops. Every day, measure how much rain there has been. Record this in a notebook over a week.

Glossary

factory building where things are made by machines

fresh water water that isn't salty

melt change from solid to liquid, such as when ice changes to water

oil a greasy liquid that burns well and is used to power cars

poison substance that can hurt or kill a living thing

recycle send off rubbish to be made into something new, instead of throwing it away

sea an area of salt water at the edge of an ocean, partly surrounded by land

soil top part of the Earth's surface, in which plants grow

stream thin, moving area of water

tentacles long thin body parts that some animals use like arms

waste rubbish or pollution

water vapour when water gets very hot, it turns from a liquid into a gas called water vapour

Index

Amazon River 11
Angel Falls 12
animals 5, 14–15, 21

clouds 8, 9

drinking water 16–17

Earth 4, 6, 14

Franz Josef Glacier 7
fresh water 7, 15

glacier 7

humans 5

ice 6–7

Lake Baikal 13
lakes 13, 15, 20

ocean 4, 8, 9, 14, 21

plants 5, 21
pollution 20–21

rain 5, 9
rivers 10–11, 12, 13, 15, 20

sea 13, 15, 20
snow 7, 9

water cycle 8–9
waterfalls 12
well 17

EXPLORE THE WORLD WITH THE POPCORN NON-FICTION LIBRARY!

- Develops children's knowledge and understanding of the world by covering a wide range of topics in a fun, colourful and engaging way
- Simple sentence structure builds readers' confidence
- Text checked by an experienced literacy consultant and primary deputy-head teacher
- Closely matched pictures and text enable children to decode words
- Includes a cross-curricular activity in the back of each book

WATCH OUT! — **Near Water** — Honor Head

HISTORY CORNER — **The Great Fire of London** — Jenny Powell

SCIENCE CORNER — **Sound and Hearing** — Angela Royston

FAMILIES — **My Mum** — Katie Dicker

GOOD FOOD — **Vegetables** — Julia Adams

PEOPLE WHO HELP US — **Police** — Honor Head

PEOPLE WHO HELP US — **Firefighters** — Honor Head

GEOGRAPHY CORNER — **Rainforests** — Ruth Thomson

A YEAR OF FESTIVALS — **Muslim Festivals** — Honor Head

HISTORY CORNER — **The Gunpowder Plot** — Jenny Powell

IN SPACE — **Planets** — Chris Oxlade

SEASONS — **Winter** — Kay Barnham

FREE DOWNLOADS!

OVER 50 TITLES TO CHOOSE FROM!

- Written by an experienced teacher
- Learning objectives clearly marked
- Provides information on where the books fit into the curriculum
- Photocopiable so pupils can take them home

www.waylandbooks.co.uk/downloads

FLAMINGO
BRAVE
A book about feeling
SCARED

Written by Sue Graves

Illustrated by Trevor Dunton

W
FRANKLIN WATTS
LONDON • SYDNEY

Flamingo was scared of lots of things.

He was scared of **spiders**.

He was scared of **the dark**.

He was scared of **loud noises**, too.

At school, he was scared of playing football.
He was scared he might kick the football
the wrong way.

He was scared of **reading out in class**
even though he was a really good reader!

7

At playtime, Flamingo was scared of playing hide-and-seek. He worried he **might get lost**.

When Flamingo got scared, he hid his head under his wing. He shivered and shook and his knees knocked together in fright. Flamingo didn't like being scared. He wanted to **be brave**.

9

On Friday, Monkey had some **exciting news**. It was his birthday the next day and everyone was invited for a sleepover in his garden.

Everyone was excited. Everyone except Flamingo.
He was scared. What if a **spider** got in the tent?
What if it got **too dark**? What if they played
hide-and-seek and he **got lost**?
Flamingo was sad.

Flamingo went to find Grandpa. Grandpa was busy in the garden. He told Grandpa his worries. He said he wished he could **be brave**. Grandpa said when he felt scared he pulled back his shoulders and lifted up his chin. He said he took a **deep breath**, too.

Flamingo pulled back his shoulders and lifted up his chin. He took a deep breath. Flamingo felt **a bit better**.

Grandpa said everyone got scared sometimes. He said when he was a little bird he was **scared of swimming**. Flamingo was surprised. He **liked swimming** very much. It was fun!

Grandpa said he thought the water **looked scary**. He said his friends helped him. He soon **loved swimming**.

Flamingo said he could ask his friends to help him.

Grandpa said that was a great idea.

15

Flamingo went to see his friends.

He told them his worries.

He said he wanted to be brave.

His friends said they would **help him**.

16

The next day, it was Monkey's party.
First of all, they played hide-and-seek.
Flamingo felt scared. He remembered what
Grandpa had said. Flamingo pulled back his
shoulders, lifted up his chin and took a deep
breath. He **felt better**.

Everyone joined in the game. Everyone had fun. And Flamingo **didn't get lost** at all.

Soon it was time for bed. Suddenly a spider ran across Flamingo's bed.

But Monkey showed Flamingo how to catch
the spider in a glass.
Flamingo **wasn't scared at all**.

It got darker and darker. Flamingo worried that it would get **too dark**. But Tiger lent him his torch and the dark **wasn't scary at all**.

22

Everyone said Flamingo was being **very brave**.

Just then, everyone heard a strange noise.
Everyone thought it was a monster **and hid**!
But Flamingo pulled back his shoulders,
lifted his chin and took a deep breath.
He peeped outside the tent.

It wasn't a monster at all. It was Monkey's big toy tractor and that wasn't scary at all. Everyone laughed and said Flamingo was **very brave**!

Flamingo was proud. He liked being brave.
It was much better than being scared!

A note about sharing this book

The *Behaviour Matters* series has been developed to provide a starting point for further discussion on children's behaviour both in relation to themselves and others. The series is set in the jungle with animal characters reflecting typical behaviour traits often seen in young children.

Flamingo is Brave
This story looks at some of the typical things that may scare children and investigates strategies for overcoming fears.

How to use the book
The book is designed for adults to share with either an individual child, or a group of children, and as a starting point for discussion.

The book also provides visual support and repeated words and phrases to build reading confidence.

Before reading the story
Choose a time to read when you and the children are relaxed and have time to share the story.

Spend time looking at the illustrations and talk about what the book might be about before reading it together.

Encourage children to employ a phonics first approach to tackling new words by sounding the words out.

After reading, talk about the book with the children:

- Talk about the story with the children. Encourage them to retell the events in chronological order.

- Talk about the things that scare the children. Point out that many of their fears are experienced by others and are especially common amongst children. Invite the children to share their fears with the group.

- Talk about how fears can be allayed. Many children like to have a night light on if they are scared of the dark. Others like to have a favourite toy to take to bed. Encourage the children to share their ideas for coping with fears. Take the opportunity to share your own childhood fears with the children and explain how you overcame them.

- Point out the strategies mentioned in the story. Grandpa got his friends to help and encourage him. He also shows Flamingo how to pull back his shoulders, lift up his chin and take a deep breath. Invite the children to stand up and try that procedure for themselves. How does it make them feel?

- As a class, invite the children to help you write a list of the things that worry them. Ask the children to suggest ways of overcoming each fear. Leave the list on display for future reference.

For Isabelle, William A, William G, George, Max, Emily,

Leo, Caspar, Felix, Tabitha, Phoebe and Harry –S.G.

Franklin Watts
First published in 2020 by
The Watts Publishing Group

Text © Franklin Watts 2020
Illustrations © Trevor Dunton 2020

The right of Trevor Dunton to be identified as the illustrator
of this Work has been asserted in accordance with the
Copyright, Designs and Patents Act, 1988.

Editor: Jackie Hamley
Designer: Cathryn Gilbert

A CIP catalogue record for this book is available
from the British Library.

ISBN 978 1 4451 7089 3 (hardback)
ISBN 978 1 4451 7090 9 (paperback)

Printed in China

Franklin Watts is a division of
Hachette Children's Books,
an Hachette UK company.
www.hachette.co.uk

FSC
www.fsc.org

MIX
Paper from
responsible sources
FSC® C104740